Shirley Shirley, whose very name is twi............mation has written a book of poems, "My Journey: Reflections on Life from a Cancer Survivor". It is a wonderful first collection full with hope, humor, and praise, prayers and the small intimacies of faith. The poems are direct, plain spoken, and unadorned. Shirley's voice is clear, true and steady, as she confronts the unknown from first diagnosis to treatment and the uncertain aftermath. She speaks openly about her fears, from her own mortality, to the intrusive nature of chemotherapy and radiation, of biopsies and incisions, to the loss of hair and dignity. Yet there is much joy, individual and communal, in these poems as she finds an invigorating spirit in memories of her Iowa childhood, in recollections of fly-fishing, cross-country skiing, and hiking in Montana's Beartooth Mountains, in gardening and knitting, and in the shared stories of family, friends, and other survivors. And, because cancer is, in her words, "not a journey that one takes alone", this book of poems will be an honest, supportive, and inspirational companion to those who must make such a journey.
-Dave Caserio, poet and member of the Humanities Montana Speakers Bureau

"Bless you for thinking of me and sending me your precious words.... They are given to you by the Lord to share with people like me...for hope and encouragement. Please keep sharing! They are a comfort.... and amazing really."
-Andrea Fisher, cancer patient

"What an inspiration your book is to me and my family. I think of it often and absolutely love it. It took me back to some of my childhood memories."
-Betty Propp, cancer patient

My Journey

REFLECTIONS ON LIFE FROM
A CANCER SURVIVOR

Shirley Shirley

WestBow
PRESS
A DIVISION OF THOMAS NELSON

Scripture taken from the Holy Bible, New International Version®. Copyright © 1973, 1978, 1984 Biblica. Used by permission of Zondervan. All rights reserved.

ISBN: 978-1-4497-4822-7 (sc)
ISBN: 978-1-4497-4823-4 (e)
ISBN: 978-1-4497-4821-0 (hc)

Library of Congress Control Number: 2012906788

WestBow Press books may be ordered through booksellers or by contacting:

WestBow Press
A Division of Thomas Nelson
1663 Liberty Drive
Bloomington, IN 47403
www.westbowpress.com
1-(866) 928-1240

Printed in the United States of America

WestBow Press rev. date: 04/26/2012

To my family: my husband, Robert (Bob) Shirley; our children, Greg Shirley, Janet Cano, Carolyn Cassata, and Diane Morledge-Hampton; our grandchildren, Jessica and Jennifer Cano, Rachel and Caleb Cassata, and Sara, Ben, Charlie, Nick, and Abbie Morledge-Hampton. You have all made my life very special.

Contents

Acknowledgments

I would like to thank Dave Caserio, poet, and Amber Ussin-Davies, social worker, for providing the class My Expression, My Voice at the Billings Clinic Cancer Center, where I was given encouragement for the past two years to write *My Journey*.

The medical staff at the Billings Clinic Cancer Center was very supportive. Dr. James Burke, my oncologist, always made me laugh, which was helpful during cancer treatment. Cheryl Grantham, my oncology nurse, made things lighter by discussing our latest knitting projects and trips to Wild Purls. Jane Hoffman helped me organize and give instruction in Hope Knit. And thanks to Alice Golden and all those involved in Montana, who make Casting for Recovery possible.

Family and friends too numerous to mention were my support. My husband was always there for me. Our daughters, Janet, Carolyn, and Diane, who traveled many miles so one of them could be with me on each chemo day, were also appreciated. Thank you, Lennyce, for the beautiful quilt, and to Helen for the scarves you lent me.

Those who have given me support and advice on my writing are also extremely appreciated. This book is not a single effort, solely of my own, but has involved so many who have been a part of my life in *My Journey*. Thank you all.

Chapter 1:
Writing Helps Me Face My Cancer Fears

The Billings Clinic Cancer Center has created a variety of classes to help the cancer patient with the support and companionship of others sharing their experiences. In the class My Expression, My Voice, led by Dave Caserio, poet, and Amber Ussin-Davies, social worker, we wrote in free-form style and then shared what we had written.

Hope Knit at Billings Clinic and Casting for Recovery provided more sharing experiences. My poems are the result of the support I was given by these organizations and the support of my family and friends.

Sharing our fears and feelings through writing helped us to understand our various struggles.

Cancer is not a journey you can take alone. It involves the support of many who are there to help you. Lasting friendships were made in these activities offered to cancer patients. I am indebted to them all.

Abbie and Shirley (Nanny) enjoying the rims in Billings, Montana

It's Cancer

It's cancer, so where do I go from here?
Diney said, "You will need a surgeon and oncologist."
Carolyn said, "You should study WebMD."
Janet said, "I'll come and be with you."
Jan sent a book.
Sue listened on the phone.
The surgeon called for a lumpectomy,
The oncologist ordered chemo,
The radiologist prescribed radiation.
I was overwhelmed
But found comfort in those who care.

My whole life flashed before me
As I sought comfort from days gone by.
Now I pray for spiritual guidance
To face my cancer treatment,
To be with those who have given me strength,
To find joy in each day.

Chemo

When my oncologist said, "Chemo,"
It brought instant fear.
My stomach was in knots.
I could not speak.

Why does this word bring such fear?
Fear like I have never known.
It is fear of the unknown,
Things I do not know that scare me.

What was I thinking when I could not speak?
My hair, will I lose my hair?
How sick will I be?
Will others need to care for me?

Will my whole life be put on hold?
Will cancer consume all my thoughts?
How will I change
When those chemicals are infused?

The Fourth Floor

I have never gone there before,
On the path that is before me.
I am nervous,
Not knowing where it leads.

But to the fourth floor I go,
Where infusions are the order,
To find my way,
Not knowing where it leads.

Many have gone before.
I'm certainly not the first.
I'll join the ones
Who have led.

May my thoughts as I go
Be centered in Christ,
Not in my treatment.
I am not alone.
The Lord said,
"Be strong and courageous.
Do not be terrified;
Do not be discouraged,
For the Lord your God will be with you
wherever you go."[1]
So I will go to the fourth floor
To face my uncertainties,
To share with those survivors,
To see where they have gone.

That my chemo mind may be clear
To think beyond myself,
To a new height of awareness
Beyond what I could have had.

May I leave behind the concerns
Of what is happening to me,
And give my thanks and praise
For all I am blessed with today.

Hair

I looked in the mirror at my bald head.
How strange—is that really me?
"It will come back in any color you want," my doctor said.
But for now, I am marked as a cancer patient.

Scarves, hats, or a wig cover my fate.
My attention in the grocery store is not on food.
All the people around me have hair.
Busily they get their groceries and go on their way.

My hair will come back, he promised,
And that it did. I removed my head covers,
And with happy surprise they all said,
"Short hair becomes you."

I looked in the mirror at my short hair.
It was so.
I like the new me.

Teeter-Totter

During chemo, I was happy to say,
"I feel almost normal today."
"Normal?" my daughter chuckled. "We aren't so sure.
Just what is normal for you?"

I was always a little on the crazy side,
With new adventures each day.
Who can tell where normal lies
when the earth goes round and round.

Up and down, all around,
How does the teeter-totter land,
In this quizzical, magical world,
Where balance is not always found?

Back to normal I hope to go,
But it will never be the same.
How will the new normal look?
Rosy, blue, green, or orange?
Each day will hold its possibilities.
To find ways we have not known,
To find the joy of being alive,
To be more thankful.

To Leave

Our writing assignment was to
Go to the dictionary, point to a word,
Then write about it.
My finger pointed to *leave*.

What an interesting word. It brings to mind
"I will never *leave* nor forsake you."[2]
This promise is made by many,
A vow not to be broken.

To *leave* behind,
Causing a void
That can weaken or strengthen.
The choice is ours to make.

What pits of despair cancer can bring.
How do I *leave* it behind?
How do I fill that void?
Climbing up out of my fears.

Taking my mind out of darkness
Where light can lead me on
To heights of new awareness,
Leaving those patterns of defeat.

Sharing

We were writing about our cancer journeys,
Each one on a different path,
Sharing where we had been,
Reliving the past.

The roads have led in different directions.
Yours took you that way and mine another.
Why is your road harder? I ask myself.
My path has been light.

Your journey was so different.
I feel your pain.
May we come together as one,
Sharing our love, tears, and joy.

My Breast

It has experienced
Examinations,
Mammograms,
Ultrasounds,
Biopsy,
Initials,
Incisions,
Chemotherapy,
Tattoos,
Radiation,
And Pain,
But it is still mine.
I am alive.

Cheryl

During my chemo infusions, Cheryl, my oncology nurse,
    would always ask me,
"Have you been to Wild Purls Knitting Shop yet?"
Then she would tell me about the socks she had been knitting
for two years, but she just couldn't turn the heel.
Her upper sock kept getting longer and longer.
I kept telling her to call me to help her,
But our schedules did not coordinate.

Also I asked Cheryl, "How long can you blame loss of
    memory on chemo?"
She replied, "As long as you want, but they won't believe you."
Her sense of humor always made me smile; what more could
    you ask for during chemo?

Hope Knit

Janet e-mailed, "What does your knitting group talk about? I
  heard on TV the ladies in California come together to knit
  so they can learn the latest gossip."

"We are Montana girls! We talk about hiking and skiing.
Lots of stories about the ski lift—falling when we got off,
staying on and riding back down while college kids booed,
crying all the way up, riding over a black diamond run," I
  answered.
We also talk about the latest yarns and patterns of course,
  but today was the best.

Today at Hope Knit, three years after her initial attempt,
  Cheryl has turned the heel and finished her sock.
Soon she has a pair, puts them on, and places her feet up on
  the table.
Cheryl had done it! We all smiled, but her smile was the
  biggest as the camera flashed.

Working together, we laughed and knitted hats for cancer
  patients
To tell them, "We understand, keep warm, and may love
  surround you."

Casting for Recovery

We were greeted with warm smiles,
Not just a normal welcome,
But by those who really cared
About the journey we were on.

Breast cancer patients brought together
To share what they had been given,
To go out and learn new skills,
Fly-casting on the river.

With my marvelous guide I cast the line,
Not one, but two trout I caught.
A dream fulfilled, losing my cares
On the stream, in the sunshine, on a Montana river.
That common bond that brought us together
Lent meaning to all we did.
The serious times, learning times, and fun times,
Expressing the struggle, giving us strength.

Casting for Recovery Catch

Bob

You have always been here for me,
Though little is sometimes said.
Your subtle humor and your evenness and calm
Give me strength.

Through years of family,
Months of cancer treatment,
You have been by my side.
Did I thank you for your support?

In addition to your encouragement
You gave me the freedom
To just be me.

Your steadfast love
Gives me inner strength,
The joy of sharing an
Everlasting love.

Chapter 2:
Journaling Also Gives Spiritual Guidance

A cancer diagnosis comes as a shock. I kept a personal journal of my fears and feelings of helplessness. In those times, I pleaded with God for answers and help. I received answers for my struggles, which I share in these poems. I separate these poems from the first chapter because a different style of writing took over, reflecting my personal seeking.

The story of Gideon gave me courage to go ahead with chemo treatments. I paraphrase these chapters where I found God speaking to me as He did to Gideon. It was a very meaningful experience.

The Psalms were also especially comforting. I found myself memorizing passages and carrying them in my head for frequent recall and comfort.

During treatment, I was given the strength to focus. Well, part of the time. I did have a chemo brain. But following treatment, I found some difficult days, which I write about in *I'm Tired*.

Most importantly, I learned to give thanks, even for the cancer, which gave me a new spiritual depth. Praise and thanksgiving came as I was given so much.

Family hike in Alkali Creek
between my chemo sessions.
Jennifer, Scott, Shirley and Abbie, Bob, Ben

Imagination

When I sit and ponder my cancer
I can be overwhelmed with fear.
My imagination takes over
And plants questions in my head.

Does imagination get me into trouble?
Does it lead me to despair?
What good can come from it?
Where do I go from here?

To choose to dwell in the unknown:
What if? Can it be?
Takes a lot of energy!
Takes a lot of energy!

To be able to trust the future
One must understand the past.
What have I been given?
What joys have come to me?

How better to dwell on these
Than fear what might happen.
Living in God's trust,
Finding strength for today.

Light

In the darkness of night
Fears can keep growing.
Where can I go?
How can I escape?

Take me out of this darkness
And let there be light.
God answered, "I am the light
of the world. Whoever follows
me will never walk in darkness,
but will have the light of life."[3]

"Every good and perfect gift
is from above, coming down from
the Father of the heavenly lights,
who does not change like shifting shadows."[4]
He is always with me.

Weakness

I feel so weak,
So many choices to make,
Not knowing how to make them,
Overcome with feelings of despair.

And in my weakness I feel I have fallen short.
Why do I feel so weak?
The Lord is my Shepherd,
He has promised to guide me.

My family and friends are here
But this is my personal struggle.
Then I am reminded, "For when I am weak, then I am
    strong."[5]
I will glory in my struggle, so that the power of Christ might
    rest upon me.
It is not my battle, but the Lord's.
Then in my feelings of abandonment, I turn to find His
    strength.

"I lift my eyes to the hills—
where does my help come from?
My help comes from the Lord,
the Maker of heaven and earth."[6]

The Trail

When the body is weak
I turn to you, oh Lord,
For inner strength I seek
To clarify your plan.

What I seek may not be your way.
Sometimes the trail is rocky and steep.
But given the strength to carry on,
I find new beauty and peace.

"We do not know what we ought to pray for,
but the Spirit himself intercedes for us
with groans that words cannot express …
The spirit intercedes for the saints in
accordance with God's will."[7]

On the trails, in the prairie and mountains,
I find an inner peace.
The waving grass and mountains tall,
Not found on city streets.
The trail is not certain,
Will it level or go up or down?
But you are my guide.
I will know the way.

Be Still

Be still my heart,
My fear be cast away,
Where faith stands alone
In You, my Lord.[8]

For fear and faith
Do not mingle,
Just as oil and water separate
And cannot be together.

I desire thy peace.
Be still my heart,
That I may find
A trust that casts away fear.

Gideon

The angel of the Lord sat under the oak tree
Near where Gideon was threshing wheat
In the safety of a winepress hiding from the Midianites.
He said, "The Lord is with you, mighty warrior."

"But sir," Gideon replied, "if the Lord is with us,
Why have the Midianites oppressed us for seven years?
The Lord has abandoned us."

The Lord answered, "Go in strength and save Israel.
Am I not sending you?"

"But Lord," Gideon replied, "how can I save Israel?
My clan is the weakest, and I am the least in my family."

The Lord answered, "I will be with you, and you will
Strike down all the Midianites together.
Peace! Do not be afraid."

Gideon obeyed God, tearing down the altar to Baal.
Then the Spirit of the Lord came upon Gideon.

To be sure, Gideon asked God twice for a sign.
First, the Lord made the fleece wet one night and dry the
    next.

So Gideon followed God, trusting Him.
With only three hundred men chosen of God,
Making a circle around the camp.

Breaking their jars, the men held the torches in their left
  hands,
And with trumpets in their right hands they shouted,
"A sword for the Lord and Gideon."
The Lord caused the men in the
Midianite camp to turn on each other
With their own swords, and they fled.[9]
God gave them the victory.

The Lord is Peace

Lord, I praise you for your name;
In my fear and discouragement give me peace.
Replace my anxieties with your love.
Help me to find my rest in your beloved Son.

You are the One who can fight my battle.
You are the Spirit of truth.
Even when I fail, you are there
To lift me up, to glorify you.

May my thoughts of self and failure
Be turned to your righteousness,
To your steadfast love and keeping,
For on you alone I depend.

Hear my cry, Oh Lord.
With thankful heart I come.
You are the answer to my struggle,
For in you is perfect peace.[10]

Sadness and Grief

I am sad and feel alone.
How do I come out of this depression?
The more I try, the worse I feel,
This cannot be the way.

I turn to Ecclesiastes
And read of those experiencing grief.
Finding that with much wisdom
Comes much sorrow.[11]

"There is a time for everything ...
A time to weep and a time to laugh,
A time to mourn and a time to dance."[12]
Wisdom preserves the life of its possessor;
Consider what God has done.[13]

"When times are good, be happy;
But when times are bad, consider:
God has made the one
As well as the other."[14]

And so I share with you,
I cannot go it alone. The Lord is there for me. He has said,
"Come to me, all you who are weary and burdened,
And I will give you rest.
Take my yoke upon you and learn from me,
For I am gentle and humble in heart,
And you will find rest for your souls.
For my yoke is easy and my burden is light."[15]
All He asks is that we come.

I'm Tired

The battle has raged for fifteen months,
Consuming all my mind.
My strength stood fast;
I was given the victory.

Now my treatments are over.
I can return to my life as before.
I keep waiting for that feeling
Of being whole again.

I expect to feel as I did before cancer,
But it is not the same.
Those around me see me healed,
But I am tired.

My body feels more vulnerable;
The concerns need sorting out.
My hormones rage and insecurities strike,
More lessons I have to learn.

I am different and always will be.
My body has gone through such change.

But Winston Churchill said,
"There is nothing wrong with change
If it is in the right direction."

So what is important now
Is which direction I take.
May I live in the moment,
Appreciating the simple joys.

The Simple Joys

What I loved before cancer is still in my heart.
Today my body is weak,
But I need to get outside,
To see, to smell, and to feel
God as I see Him in His creation.

I remember how it used to be.
The wild flowers along the path,
The streams rushing down,
Hiking in the mountains.

I'll gain my strength
And return to the Beartooths
To hike with my friends,
To eat lunch along the shore.

Losses

I was still grieving the losses
That cancer and age have caused within me.
I felt weighted down,
Like soggy piles of leaves.

When suddenly
I was given a gift.
Esther in the Old Testament said,
"If I perish, I perish!"[16]
She had the courage
To see beyond herself.

And so I said,
"If I have losses, I have losses!"
And suddenly the weight fell from my shoulders.
I could again live in the joy of the Lord.

Praise

I was walking down 17th Street
With the mountains in view
And my heart sang out,
"This is the day the Lord has made;
Let us rejoice and be glad in it."[17]

You are the theme of my praise.
I will praise You all day long,
In the valleys and on the mountaintops.
I will dance and sing of His goodness.

The angels join me with
Harp, lyre, strings, flute, trumpet,
And the clashing of cymbals.
I will praise the Lord with a loud voice.[18]

When Doors Do Not Open

When answers do not come
And the way is hard to find
How do I seek the path?
I do not know the way.

I wonder and ask
For an answer,
Relief for my pain,
A way out; an escape.
Ask and it shall be given.

When doors are closed
I must continue
On to seek the path,
The right one for today.
Seek and you will find.

It takes faith to be still and listen.
I continue to knock at the door.
The answer will come in time
Showing me the one that opens.[19]
Knock and it will be opened.

Your Face

The beauties of this earth,
The sun, moon, and stars
Will be needed no more
When your face I see.[20]

The majestic brilliance of Jesus,
In all His splendor and glory,
Will be greater than sunlight on snow,
More pure than crystal waters.[21]

I wait for the day I see You,
Keep my focus on your face,
On your perfect brilliance,
On your saving, unchanging grace.

Chapter 3:
My Childhood Gives Me Strength

In writing class led by Dave Caserio and Amber Ussin-Davies at the Billings Clinic Cancer Center, in addition to writing about our cancer experience, we were given the assignment to write about our childhood. After writing "The Chicken House," I continued to write about this time in my life.

Because cancer so consumes the mind, it was refreshing to look back on the carefree times of my youth. It was a great release and helped me appreciate what I had been given. In childhood I learned to love the out-of-doors—and also cats. These have stayed with me my entire life, giving me strength.

Jack, Dick, and Shirley Kintner in their
big back yard in Des Moines, Iowa.

My Legacy

Where do I come from?
How do I know?
Heat of the summer,
Coldness of snow?

Why do I enjoy the garden?
My father taught me so.
My mother loved to bake and can.
The kitchen was her home.

In springtime, I gathered Lilies-of-the-Valley.
Summer meant picnics at Walnut Woods.
Fall brought homemade tomato soup and grape jelly.
Winter was for making snowmen and snow forts.

New View

The leaves are falling from the trees,
Opening a window for me to see
Far beyond
To the mountains covered with snow.

The snow is cold but deep.
In caves the bears sleep.
It is a time of rest.
It is a time to remember.

Snowmen, sledding, and skating,
Being hit by a snowball, unaware,
Catching a snowflake on my mitten,
Sliding across the slippery ice.

What fun we had, my dog Whip and I,
Skiing down the hills at Greenwood Park,
Whip barking and running ahead—
Me gliding close behind.

Growing Up in Des Moines

Growing Up in Des Moines
We had the best of both,
Living in the city, but near the countryside.
Our acreage gave us room to explore,
To build forts and hike through fields and streams.
Once Jack fell in the stream when he dared to walk a log.
He was cold when we took him out of the water,
So we made a fire and dried his clothes.

The willows way back in the cornfield
Would attract my dog, my brothers, and me.
We would cut trails and rooms, and make willow furniture.
On a rainy year we even took a boat out there.

In the natural world of our youth
We could climb trees without fear.
We'd shoot baskets, pick apples, and feed the chickens,
Or we would go on the city bus downtown.

We would ride the swaying trolley cars on rails
Or the curb liners on fat wheels
That sometimes made me sick.
Since my mother did not drive a car,
We rode them quite a bit.
She took me downtown on the bus
To Kresges, Woolworths, and Younkers,
Where we would eat *rarebit* sandwiches
And have our photos taken in a booth.

The Chicken House

I am a child again back in the chicken house.
My two brothers are shelling corn.
As we turn the handle the cob goes through the sheller;
The wooden box fills with golden kernels of corn.

One of thirteen cats comes from the corn crib,
Curling up next to me,
Purring while I pet her,
While Cutie is nursing her kittens.

My father liked to have the cats
In the corn crib to keep down the mice.
My mother also gave us bread and milk
To feed them. Cat food didn't exist back then.

The smell of chickens and straw comes from the next room.
A hen lets out a loud cluck. Another egg is laid for me to
    collect.
I reach into the nest in a row of wooden boxes on the wall.
It is still warm when I place the egg in the bucket.

The chicken house was a fun place,
A place for us kids to hang out,
A safe place away from the world,
Where we could laugh, and play, and be silly.

Our Yard

We had a big yard when I was little.
It even had a football field,
Out in the back by the chicken house,
Next to the grapevines, fruit trees, and vegetable gardens.
The basketball hoop was by the garage.
I liked to shoot baskets
And play HORSE with my brothers.

There were always boys in our yard.
There were lots and lots of boys.
Once they let me play army with them.
Orders were shouted out: "Right Face."
I couldn't remember which way to turn,
So I didn't get to march with them anymore.

There were no girls around,
Just lots of boys,
And cats.
I liked playing with the cats.

One day Jack threw a baseball bat at Dick.
Jack said the spanking was worth it.

The Big Yellow House

It was built in Des Moines about 1904 when my father was a
  baby,
The big yellow house. It was a farm house when he was a boy,
An acreage when I was growing up in the forties,
And then just a city lot after World War II.

It stood tall at 5100 Hickman, on Highway 6, paved in brick
  years ago.
My bedroom was in the middle upstairs. The bedrooms on
  each end had
Walk-in closets, but mine had none, so my father built me a
  little one.
In my bedroom I had a little white radio, and there was a
  really pretty perfume bottle high on my mother's dresser.

Our house didn't have a television until I was in junior high.
On Sunday night I would listen to the program *Inner
  Sanctum.*
It would start with a scary creaking noise of a door opening.

The upstairs had no heat in the winter, no warming pans
  either.
There was a coal bin room by the furnace in the basement.
Sometimes I had to wait on the basement steps for Dad to get
  home from Northwestern Bell
To give me a spanking.
He installed switchboards for the telephone company.

The floor register next to the oven in the kitchen was a good
  place to get warm.

My mother spent a lot of time there baking, cooking and
  canning.
She would listen to her radio in the kitchen, to *Kitchen
  Klatter.*
The ladies from Shenandoah would chat and give good
  recipes.
Just off the kitchen was a bathroom with a glass window in
  the door.
When my parents were gone, my brother threw a shoe in
  there at me.
I slammed the door and the shoe came through the window.

Between the living room and the dining room was an arch.
Under it we played marbles on the little rug.
The big radio in a wooden case was in the living room.
Dick, Jack and I would lie on the rug in front by the radio
And listen to the *Lone Ranger Rides Again* with Tonto.
That arch became a stage on Christmas Eve for the kids
To perform our Christmas program for the adults who were
  in the living room.
Then on Christmas in the dining room, the big table under
  the chandelier,
Which was saved for special occasions, would be set with
  china and silver
And piled high with Mom's cooking.

After living in the big yellow house for ninety years, my
  father finally agreed to leave his home and come live close
  to me in Eldora. He had kept it brightly painted for many
  years. The gardens were outstanding. Even today some still
  recall his big round canna bed next to the big yellow house.

Painting of the Big Yellow House in Des
Moines done by Shirley Shirley

The Cribbage Board

He made it himself from a piece of plywood.
First, my father cut out a ten-inch circle,
And then he drilled three even rows.
Each row had 120 holes, marked off in fives.
Broken colored toothpicks would serve for pegs.
He covered the back with green felt.

How he loved to play.
I wish the board could talk.
At Christmas we even had tournaments.
The winner held the trophy.

When Stuart moved from his house,
Where he had lived for ninety years, in Des Moines,
The cribbage board came with him
To be displayed on his kitchen table.

I would go down nearly every day.
He would serve me a Diet Coke and a chocolate-
    marshmallow cookie
To enjoy while we played cribbage.
He counted his hand, "15-2, 15-4, and a pair is six."
The terms stink hole, skunked, and double skunked
Always carried a fascination for all my children and
    grandchildren.

Each time I had chemo
A daughter came for support,
Bringing Grandpa's cribbage board
To peg our game and shorten my four-hour sessions.
From generation to generation
The board will be handed down.
The tradition will not die,
This bonding of family ties.

Grandma Nellie

Her name was Nellie Tissington Barr.
She lived just one block away.
How I loved to go and see her.
She always seemed to be home.

Grandma Nellie kept cake and cookies in a low cupboard
    drawer.
She made them from scratch, no recipe, of course.
Then off she would send me to Harvey's Grocery,
Just two blocks south, with an extra dime—just for me.

Sometimes I would help her pick raspberries,
But most of the time we played games.
I got really good at Chinese checkers.
She loved the carom board best.

Grandma Nellie and Grandpa George came for holidays.
With linens on the table and fine china too,
Roast beef, Yorkshire pudding, Jell-O salad,
And mile-high lemon chiffon pie were the best.

What a gift to be so close,
To share these memorable times.
Sixty or seventy years have passed,
But I still see us together.

Grandpa George

He lived just a block from us,
In a little white house he had built.
Before retirement Grandpa had been a carpenter.

He chewed tobacco.
You didn't want to sit behind him in the car.

When he no longer had a driver's license
He would walk to Franklin Avenue
And ride the city bus to the Union Hall
For a game of pinochle.

It seems like in those days
He was always going to funerals.
Grandma would come to our house with him
Only when my father drove her the one block to our house.

When you asked George Smouse Barr,
"What nationality are you?"
He would say, "I'm a Duke's Mixture."
I guess that meant a little of everything.

One day he caught a big catfish in the Des Moines River.
He put on his best suit and brought that fish to our place for
   us to take his picture.

My Other Grandma

She sat in her wheelchair.
She did not smile.
I remember little.
She sat there every day.

The day I broke her rubber plant
She was very cross with me.
"Don't worry, Grandma," I said,
"When Daddy comes home, he will fix it."

Then one day her wheelchair was gone.
Grandma was no longer there.
My mother told me,
"She went to another house to live."

Only once I remember visiting her.
Up the stairs we climbed.
Where all the bedrooms were full
Of lots of old people in lots of beds.

Y Camp at Boone, Iowa

What joy was brought to my youth,
Eight summers in all
Going to Y Camp on the inter-urban train,
Over the high bridge to be with the girls.

Our cabin was on the hillside.
Up the steep steps we would climb,
Where strength was built
To last a lifetime.

We sang in the mess hall, washed dishes,
Went to archery, crafts, swimming, and tennis.
We even had outdoor toilets.

My favorite place of all was
Cleopatra's bathtub, a spot in the nearby stream.
After cookouts, overnights, and campfires,
The final one would bring tears.
Back to Des Moines, to my cats and brothers
For more adventures with them.

The High Bridge

Teenagers at the Boone Y Camp
Out on a hike,
Going to the high railroad bridge.
It was the highest of its kind.

Walking the tracks we kept our balance.
No railing on the sides to catch us.
What can we do that would be really wild?
This bridge is calling for danger!

"I know, we'll take off our shirts
And take pictures of us in our bras.
Stopping on the middle,
At the highest part of the bridge."
The train whistle did not come.
We didn't even have to run in terror for our lives.
We just kept laughing.
Silly Girls we were.

Chapter 4:
My Family Teaches Me Courage

Marriage, careers, and having children have many difficult challenges, as well as joys.

I could relate to cancer in the same way, finding helpful resources from my marriage and children to conquer the hard times with moments of love and joy.

Children offer so many rewards and memories. Their future unfolds before us in wonderful ways, just as my journey with cancer did. Our children have taught me courage.

When I was diagnosed with cancer, one of my first thoughts was, *We only have a year until our Fiftieth Anniversary. I hope I am there to celebrate with my husband and family.* And I was.

Our wedding and fifty year
anniversary invitation

Our four children; Greg, Janet, Carolyn, and
Diane at our fiftieth anniversary

Family hike in the Beartooth
Mountains as an anniversary event

Fifty Years Have Passed

Robert Shirley and Shirley Kintner
On August 7, 1960, our wedding vows were said,
Making us Robert and Shirley Shirley.
Robert was seeking a location to practice dentistry.
Eldora, Iowa, seemed to be the one,
With Pine Lake and the Iowa River,
For canoeing and rafting.

Diapers were our theme of the sixties,
Greg born in '61, Janet in '62,
Then Carolyn in '65 and Diane in '67.
It all comes together.

The small town had its merits,
Numerous school activities they could enjoy,
But best of all they thrived in the outdoors,
Building forts from mattress springs and such.

Summer parades brought blue ribbons
But the one not forgotten is when they were Snow White and
the Seven Dwarfs with the Schafer kids. Legs painted with
    red tempura—
An itch they will always remember.
On to colleges, marriages, and nine grandchildren; the years
    have flown so fast.
And now we all are gathered to celebrate the fifty years that
    have passed.

Pine Lake and the Iowa River

Our four children Greg, Diane, Carolyn, and Janet on
a hike at Pine Lake State Park near Eldora, Iowa

We had chosen a good place for our children to grow up
Along the Iowa River, next to Pine Lake State Park.
The paths opened to new discoveries;
You could hike them all year long.

In the spring all sorts of woodland wildflowers would bloom:
Hepaticas, delicate and pink, trillium and bloodroot.
Anemone, toothwort, and spring beauty.
The children loved Dutchman's-breeches and Jack-in-the-
   pulpit.

In the summer when the blooms were gone,
We would find wild blackberries, gooseberries, and
   raspberries.

After eating them we would go for a swim
Or take the raft to the river.

By fall, when leaves turned orange, red, and gold.
We found a prairie
Where we could harvest
Native seed to plant along the roadside.

Winter had many sports:
Ice skating, skiing, and sledding.
Houses appeared on the lake where
They drilled their fishing holes.

Christmas in Yucatan

Our children were five, seven, nine, and eleven years old.
With Partners of the Americas we would travel
To a world so different from our own.

We boarded the airplane, each child with a zippered bag
I had made to carry their special belongings.
From crisp snowy air to warm heavy air,
We were greeted with spicy aromas.

On our first night in Merida, Yucatan, Mexico
At the Flamingo Hotel,
The children swam outside in winter
And went to a Rotarian festival.

Then off on the bus along with chickens in cages,
The people with lovely dark skin and colorful clothes
Gave us an introduction to a life other than our own.

At the village, our children slept in hammocks
In the doctor's white stucco home,
Near the mission hospital and huts of the villagers.
All day they played while we provided dentistry to the Mayan
    people.
Translations were made from English, to Spanish, to Maya.

The indigenous people were warm, and wore white clothing
    so bright.
Their embroidery was magnificent,
Their gold medallion jewelry exquisite.

Boys carried home wood for the fire,
While girls carried ground corn from the mill on their heads.
A Mayan lady made us tamales baked in an underground fire,
Brought to us with love and wrapped in banana leaves.

We left the village to spend Christmas by the sea
On the Island of Isla Mujeres, with sandy white beaches
And clear blue-green waters, and crashing waves,
Where turtles and sharks swam in pens.
The food, sun, and surf gave us delight,
Giving us thoughtful hearts as we returned to winter.

Chapter 5:
Gardening Gives Me Joy

My husband and I both grew up with gardens, so it was a natural thing to cultivate our own and see the growth and change over our forty-seven years in the black Iowa soil of Eldora, Iowa.

We had many perennial flowers and fruit, but I loved most planting the annual vegetable garden. Feeling the life of the seed in your hands and smelling the newly turned soil spoke of renewal and hope. It brought satisfaction harvesting the produce God had given us.

And so it is with cancer. The seed of our needs is planted, and it is gratifying to see the results of all the ways God has provided as I mature on the journey, giving me joy.

Sara in the garden with Shirley (Nanny) in Eldora, Iowa

Planting

The old hand plow was used
To push and turn the rich soil over,
Preparing for planting.
The smell was earthy and clean.

With rakes we leveled the soil,
Then placed a line to keep our rows straight.
A row was made with the hoe.

Seeds planted by hand in just the right place,
Radishes, lettuce, peas, carrots, beets, and beans.
Then with the hoe I would cover the seeds.

Each day we would look with anticipation,
Watching for the sprouts to emerge,
To rise above the soil.

Beans

I became so enamored with beans that spring,
Planting twelve kinds in the rich Iowa soil,
Waiting and watching for them to grow,
Green sprouts rising from the earth.

Sprouts rapidly rose, sending out
Tendrils to cling to the poles.
Four long rows in all,
Growing in our backyard garden.

By fall the beans hung heavy under the leaves.
I felt for their large, crisp pods.
Holding them in my hands I felt
New life within the seeds.

When the baskets were full, I carried them in,
Waiting for a quiet, snowy day
To shell the colorful beans from their pods,
To view, to eat, and to plant some again.

Compost

Before people were aware of the term compost,
Bob was saving wasted food and plant matter.
He would dig garbage into trenches
And pile the fallen leaves into large holding pens.

Over the years the compost made a transformation;
The clay turned to loam.
It was a continual recycling and renewing,
Giving him fruit for his labor.

With respect for what it had been,
Bob continued to build the soil.
Year by year it was restored—
The life in our garden.

Bob's Hobby

He would get out the splitter
And run the logs through.
He chopped and sawed as the chips flew,
Until each log was cut just right.

The pile of firewood would grow,
Stacked high in a neat row,
Waiting for winter.

And when winter came,
He would build his fire,
Filling the house with its aroma.
Flames leapt and danced,
Delighting us each day.

Then back out into the snow
He would go with the ashes,
To collect firewood again,
and so it went all winter.

The Wheelbarrow

It must have been as old as us,
Our heavy steel wheelbarrow,
The sturdiest I had ever seen.

We don't know where it came from.
It had been given to us.
Perhaps it had been used in construction.
There was cement stuck inside.

In the yard, it made a presence.
We would fill it to the brim;
Grandkids, pumpkins, and apples,
It could carry the load within.

Workhorse that it was,
We could always depend on it
Around our yard in Eldora.

The wheel barrow by Bob's wood pile.

My Gardens

For forty-seven years my gardens were my joy.
I weeded, planted, and transplanted.
Added benches and pots and frog decorations.

And then we moved away,
Before the great storm came.
With hail and wind it leveled everything.

On our return, the change was depressing.
And then in the backyard next to where the pond had been
I saw yellow daffodils in bloom—
The ones I had planted.

Chapter 6:
Sports Build My Endurance

Exercise has always been a part of my life. I especially enjoy any sport that takes me outdoors.

On hikes by myself I can meditate and appreciate the details of nature. In group sports I am able to share the enjoyment of being together.

Being active has helped give me endurance and a way to handle the stress of cancer. I tried to get outside and walk every day when I felt I had enough strength.

More poems about my enjoyment of an active life in Montana follow.

Shirley hiking at Meeteetse Palisades Trail in the Beartooth Mountains

A Day of Cross-Country Skiing in Iowa

The temperature rose to double digits.
I layered my clothing and grabbed my ski equipment.
Arriving at Pine Lake I saw fifteen new fishing houses.
I fit my boots into my skis and clamped the toes down.
The sun danced on the snowflakes, reflecting colors like
    diamonds.
Following a snowmobile trail, I crossed the lake to the beach
    house.
I wiped cold tears from my eyes when the wind hit my face.
All was quiet.
Tree trunks on the shore appeared grayish-brown with
    feather tips.
I skied down the path under the warmth of their branches.
Then a hawk glided horizontally through the trees.
I soon heard loud noises of crows defending their territory.
The gray and white scene turned to color as I focused on the
    oak leaves,
Red bush twigs, red berries, and some orange bittersweet.
Then I heard the snow crunching under my skis.
I saw tracks from a tiny mouse next to deer tracks along the
    trail.
I came to the dam and listened to water flowing from the
    frozen lake.
Then I passed two large trees that beavers had gnawed.

They had abandoned them, biting off more than they could
  chew.
I returned across the lake and checked the catch of the day.
My hands in my mittens were warm with perspiration
As I returned to our home on the other side of the river.

Register's Annual Great Bike Ride across Iowa

Bicycles were not meant to have motors.
That's what our two feet were made for,
To pedal a bike across Iowa,
In the heat, wind, and rain of July.

Ten thousand cyclists with permits would gather at
The Missouri River to dip the back tire in,
Then ride across to the Mississippi to
Joyfully christen the front tires.

Lines for Porta Potties were long, so
We found the corn fields a good substitute.

Along the way, we had pork chops in the morning,
Homemade sandwiches and cookies galore.
Church ladies ready to pile plates high, followed by music on
  the square.
Then we would put up our tents, seven days in a row.

I peddled, and peddled, and peddled
Up hills, coasting down
With oh so many cyclists
RAGBRAI, how could I ever forget?

Chapter 7:
Moving to Montana Gives New Perspectives

In Iowa, I studied the tallgrass prairie after a bicycle accident. As a volunteer, I helped collect native seed to be planted on roadsides. This was great therapy while I was healing. I loved the feeling of the seeds in my hands and went on to sketch the plants and publish *Restoring the Tallgrass Prairie* (University of Iowa Press, 1994). The endurance of the plants through great root systems and other survival techniques spoke to me of my heritage.

I loved Pine Lake and the Iowa River near our town of Eldora, Iowa. Our family spent a lot of time there, and I painted the scenes of nature in watercolor and pastel.

In retirement we wanted to be close to five of our nine grandchildren who lived in Billings, Montana. So after months of cleaning out our home of forty-seven years, a challenge in itself, Bob and I and our cat Bunny made the move. What a joy it was being with them and hiking in the Beartooth Mountains. We continued to explore the areas of Montana and Wyoming and its many natural wonders, such as Yellowstone, The Tetons, and Glacier Park.

Cancer we do not choose, but we can choose how we are going to deal with it. It gives us a new perspective on life.

Pastel painting of an Iowa Prairie done by Shirley Shirley

From Iowa to Montana

In 2008, we left the Iowa prairies for the Montana
   Mountains,
     Leaving green prairies for blue skies and mountains.

Level quiet creeks were replaced
     With crashing white water streams in the mountains.

In Iowa I biked many miles,
     And now I hike the mountains.

My past has deep prairie roots,
     My present the high snowy mountains.

Perseverance of the Tallgrass Prairie

I knew so little about the tallgrass prairie
Even though I had grown up in the midst of its history,
Where hundreds of flower species have bloomed,
And grasses grew tall enough to tickle a buffalo's belly.

Somehow I missed learning of the prairie in my school years.
Then, as an adult, I met those who cared about its demise.
We sought out the little native remnants,
Catalogued and sketched the remaining species.

The prairie had survived for centuries,
But recently only little patches have escaped the steel plow.
Farmers have tilled the depth of loam created by the prairie
To feed the hungry world.

How did the prairie survive
Fires, winds, heat, and drought?
It was these elements of nature
That made it so resilient, so strong.

In my gardens, I honor these plants.
They grow in their rightful place.
They dance with wandering colors, shapes, and textures.
They have a spirit all their own.

Transitions

Living in the moment is good
But I also appreciate my past,
For it brings strength and joy
With faith to face the future.

We think little of our environment
When we are growing up
But my childhood memories are good—
Of the natural wonders on our city acreage.
Then my adulthood on the prairie
Near the Iowa River and Pine Lake
Reassured me that all was well
On my many outdoor adventures.

Now in my senior years,
A new vista I have to explore,
The beautiful mountains of Montana
And our grandchildren's exciting ways.

The transitions I have made
Continue to bring me pleasure.
Even as I get older,
I will find strength in my past.

After the Fire

After the fire
New life springs forth,
Beneath the blackened trees
A carpet of flowers blooms.

Yellow, blue, lavender, pink, and white,
An array of colors is seen.
That one is fireweed,
Among the carpet of bloom.

Year by year,
The evergreens return,
Until the mountainside
Is again bright green.

It took the fire
To wipe the mountain clean,
So the full carpet of flowers
Could come and be seen.[22]

Mountain Stream

Rushing down from icy mountain tops,
The stream leaps over and around rocks,
Creating white, splashing water,
So clear and cold.
Searching for what lies ahead,
Rivers that go to the ocean,
Rushing to the sea.
The beauty of these waters
Give me reason to praise,
For God has promised to all who believe
Streams of living water to flow within him.[23]
God in me! How exciting that is.

Waterfall

The waterfall made no sound.
It stood in perfect silence,
With majestic formal pattern.

Winter had frozen it solid.
Nowhere could it go.
It remained a sculpted beauty.

When winter was over,
The sun did its job,
So the waterfall continued falling.

It splashed and sparkled,
Happy to be free,
Flowing with sounds of victory.

Soaring

Did you ever go up the mountain
And climb on a boulder to sit,
To be still and empty,
Waiting to be filled?

If the vessel is emptied
There is room for filling.
The imagination can grow,
Open to new beginnings.

Like a bird
Soaring in the air,
Then gliding and hovering
Until its vision is focused.

Then quietly on the mountain
All sound is hushed,
Breathing is slowed,
Bringing peace within.

Rock Creek along the Lake Fork Trail
in the Beartooth Mountains

East Rosebud on a November Day

Hellroaring Falls in East Rosebud
hiked to as described in this poem

Up the mountain I hiked with the Red Lodge hikers,
Equipped with backpack and walking sticks,
We were setting out for a day of adventure.

Over the log-covered stream we tested our balance, one by
  one.
Then up the path came our three dog companions, all leaping
  and frisky.

My Journey

Oh to leave the world behind and find such pleasure.

The leaves have left the aspens, standing tall and white.
And looking up we spied three grouse quietly watching us,
Seeming to soak up the warm sun before the first snowfall.

Then my eyes were drawn to the green and purple shadows
   far to the left.
Across the ravine I saw the colorful new evergreens growing
   twelve years after the fire.
Such bright colors were unusual on a November day.

We sat on some logs on the rocky beach by the cold, icy,
   flowing creek,
Opened our lunch sacks and continued to chatter.
The view of the cold stream and colorful mountain continued
   to draw me.

After lunch we were invited to cross the stream to go see
   Hellroaring Falls.
Six out of fourteen of us removed our shoes and socks to
   make the crossing.
With cold water up to our knees, our feet were numb to the
   rocks within the stream.

Up the steep path, up and up we went.
I said to my friend, "Do you realize we're behind the
   extremely experienced hikers?
What were we thinking?"

At last, the sound of the waterfall was greater than my
   beating heart.
There was so much water coming over the falls in November.
Such a special reward it was, a climax to our day of hiking.

Then on our return, a shout went out, "Look down there—
   two moose!"
How strong and gallant they appeared before my eyes,
In the wild, free to wander.

Back at the cabin, we met the other eight,
Telling of hungry bears who were about to hibernate.
Fellowship ended our beautiful day and hiking season in the
   Beartooth Mountains.

The Bear

We were hiking in the Beartooth Mountains,
Large bells jingled from her backpack,
Close to her large can of bear spray.
I asked, "Have you ever seen a bear?"

"No, but look on the trail,
That is bear scat,
And it looks fresh," she said.
"They can't be far away."

I'm not sure if I am ready
For an encounter.
And yet, to see a bear in the wild
Caught my fancy.
What would we do if one appeared?

Up the rugged mountain
We went, on the trail
Between the pines,
But no bear appeared.

Back in Red Lodge, we stopped for gas.
And then I saw it.
There, in town, was a bear crossing the highway.

On a Snowy Day at Riverfront Park

(The photo on the cover was taken the day of this hike)

I sit on this rock
Watching the river flowing,
Weaving under the ice, unseen,
Then resurfacing and flowing on.

The mountains are covered with snow
Where motorbikes scaled them last summer.
These mountains sit in stillness,
Absorbing the winter's sun.

Then my skis glide along,
Collecting melting snow.
With a jerk I am slowed down,
But I lunge onward up the trail.

The cool air refreshes me.
The scenery is serene.
Skiing with my daughter,
Sharing the day together.

Molt

It was the middle of December on a sunny day
When Bob and I headed west out of Billings on the Molt Road,
To the number-one rated tourist attraction, according to our
    visiting friends.

To our left, the foothills had a little snow
And beautiful purple shadows.
Beyond the foothills rose the dark blue snow-covered
    Beartooth Mountains.
We came upon the plains where golden grass waved in the
    breeze.
Large round bales of hay stood in the field, later to be fed to
    the black cows nearby.

Beyond Molt, we could see the Crazy Mountains standing
Tall in the west, covered with even more snow than the
    Beartooths.
The town of Molt seemed to have more grain bins than
    houses.
The only large building read "HARDWARE" on the brick
    facing.
It had been remodeled into the Prairie Winds Cafe,
Advertising home cooking, soups and pies.
It was well decorated with chickens in the front windows.
A chicken also stood on the top of a paper towel stand
In the center of all the uniform light-pine tables.
Tall ladders were still attached to the shelves going up to the
    ceiling.
Four grey-haired gentlemen were tuning up their guitars.

An old tin sign on the wall read, "DRINK COFFEE: DO
STUPID THINGS FASTER WITH
MORE ENERGY!" I asked the waitress the population of Molt
and she said, "Twenty or Sixteen."
Plates piled high with bacon, eggs, toast, and hash browns
were being served,
But I had the pecan roll in mind, loaded with brown sugar
and pecans along with
My bottomless cup of coffee.
The music started with western tunes, then went to "Silver
Bells" and
"White Christmas." A mouth harp was added to the four
guitars.
We finished and got up to make room for those still standing
in line.
And that is just how it always is in Molt
On a Saturday morning.

The Shopping Cart

For fifty years, Bob was a father, husband, and dentist,
And I a mother, housewife, shopper, nurse, and artist.
We followed our roles
And all—well almost all—got done.

Now we are in retirement,
Where there is a blending of roles.
My space is being invaded,
Sharing household tasks is a new function for me.

The grocery shopping is another thing,
"I'll push the cart," he says.
It seems to be a manly thing.
Off he goes, where no one knows.

I bring some groceries to him and ask,
"Where is the cart?"
"It was here somewhere," he says.
We continue to look.

Then coming toward us
Is an elderly man alone with little expression,
Pushing a cart toward us.
The contents look familiar.

"Could this belong to you?" he asked.
"Yes, I do believe it is ours."
To which he replied, "I got the cart to the cash register
And found the contents strange."
Then we helped him find his cart.

Shirley Shirley

Home we go together
Sorting groceries, from the car to carry.
I think I'm beginning to get it,
Climbing the stairs together.

The Shepherd's Wagon

Until I moved to Montana, I was not aware of the Shepherd's
  wagon.
The two I have seen were magical red homes, intended to be
  pulled by horses,
To take the shepherd around the green pastures to care for
  his sheep.

The wagons gave protection, a place to prepare food and to
  sleep.
In return, the shepherd could care for,
Pasture, and tend to his flock.

His rod and staff protected them,
As did the Word and Spirit that protected the Shepherd.
He covered their heads with oil to keep off flies.
His direction liberated and comforted them.

Together they traveled in sunshine and rain
On smooth, rough, and dangerous terrain.
His love exceeded all their demands
The sheep's welfare was his relentless desire.[24]

Chapter 8:
Grandchildren Give Me Hope

Any grandparent can agree on what a blessing grandchildren are. You can enjoy them without all the responsibility. The things they say and do take your mind into wonderful places.

When cancer is forever on your mind, there is nothing like grandchildren to take you to a better place. My grandchildren have given me hope for the future.

Our nine grandchildren: Jennifer, Sara, Abbie, Charlie, Nick, Caleb, Rachel, Jessica, and Ben, gathered at our Fiftieth Anniversary.

The Shark

Our first grandchildren, not one but two,
Jennifer and Jessica, twins growing up in the Yucatan,
So far from our Iowa home.
Where ocean tides meet swaying palms.

Flamingos, blue waters, and pyramids,
Warm days in the sun.
As the years went by, you both learned to scuba dive.
So we decided to have a three-generation dive.

The boat took us through the waters near Cozumel,
Equipped with gear and tanks.
Over the side we plunged, down into the clear, deep waters,
Where colorful coral and tropical fish abound.
We were swimming along when
Suddenly a big shark came right toward us.
My eyes got big, but he looked the other way.
He swam right around me.

It was miraculous to feel so included in the colorful world
Of coral, fish, turtles, eels, stingrays, and one enormous
    shark.

The "Quirrels"

Rachel was about three years old
When we went on a boat to the island
In Long Island Sound.

We visited the lighthouse
And walked around.
Then Grandpa found some big acorns
And put them in his pocket to take home.

The next morning at breakfast,
His acorns were on the table.
Rachel said, "Sometimes my mother lets
Me feed the 'quirrels.' They would love your acorns."

"But I am going to take them home to Iowa
To grow them in my yard," he said.

"Well, Grandpa, maybe you should think about the
Feelings of the 'quirrels,'" she said.
And so he did.

The Core of Her Body

Caleb and Rachel, our New York grandchildren,
Went with us on the boat
To the Statue of Liberty just before 9/11.
From the statue we stood high above the water
Where many had passed, coming to America
To follow their dreams and begin a new life.

And then we went to the Intrepid,
Docked on Manhattan's harbor,
Reminders of war—of protection.

We continued to ride the subway
And take in other parts of the city,
Feeling safe, enjoying the day.
Our hearts were light as we watched
The minstrels on street corners.

Strolling under the skyscrapers,
We gave the twin towers a passing glance
Amid the massive Manhattan structures.

Sara

The twins were eight when you were born
In Charleston, South Carolina.
You've traveled far and wide,
Flying to many destinations.

The one I most remember is when your father
Flew you and your mother in a Cessna 172
From Billings, to Iowa, to the East Coast and back.
You were only two or three.

In Iowa, we would play Stampin' and Showdown Yahtzee
While the younger kids took their naps.
You worked hard for your prize robe
Those summers in Branson.

From Valedictorian to college campus
To California you have gone.
We love it when you join us again,
To hear how your life is unfolding.

Benjamin Stuart

You were born the year my father died,
So, for your middle name, you were christened with his:
  Stuart.
Growing up in Virginia, Missouri, and Montana,
You traveled far and wide.

Remember that time in Missouri?
You told me,
"I have lost my Game Boy,
And that doesn't mean I can't find it."

When we went to Virginia City
And Abbie was just a toddler,
You didn't let her out of your sight.
She could not wander.

In MathCounts you were a whiz,
High honors in Montana competitions,
To us you are the best,
Our thoughtful, dependable Ben.

The Needles Go Up and Down

Abbie was watching me knitting.
"I want to learn to knit," she said.

"Maybe you need to be older," I replied.

"But I want to learn now,
To make the needles go up and down."

And so we gave it a try,
But the needles didn't go up and down.

"In a few years you will be able to learn.
But for now, I'll make you a sweater
To start kindergarten."

"Will you make me mittens, too?" she asked.
And so she sat and watched
The needles go up and down,
Creating garments just for her.

The Climbing Tree

As soon as the car arrived in Eldora from Kansas City,
The grandchildren would jump out
And head for the climbing tree.

We planted the crab apple years ago,
And by then its branches had graceful twists and turns.
A step up its trunk gave them a start up the tree.

Going up was fun, but coming down was not.
Like a cat up a tree, they screamed for help.
Once down, up they would go again
Into their favorite climbing tree.

Snow in July

The Morledge-Hampton grandchildren and their
mother in the alpine tundra near Gardner Lake in the
Beartooth Mountains, 11,000 feet elevation.

Our four grandchildren, Ben, Charlie, Nick, and Abbie,
All fastened their seatbelts.
Sara was off to college.
The van headed south from Billings to Red Lodge.
Then we drove the mountain switchbacks.
"These beautiful mountains are Montana," their mother said.
"Yeah, Mom, It's just Montana," they replied.

"But people come from all over to drive the Beartooth
   Highway."
Then we stopped to feed the chipmunks,
And some people from Japan were taking photos.
We drove on up to Gardner Lake.
Wildflowers were blooming in mass.
The Alpine climate kept them small and dainty.
We sat among them and ate our lunch,
With the lake and snowcapped mountains in view.
Abbie took off her shoes and walked in the snow,
And of course the boys had a snowball fight.
What an adventure it was
Playing in the snow in July,
High in the Beartooth Mountains.

Faces in the Rims

I am not alone hiking in the rims.
Faces look down at me
With tales of days gone by;
The stories they could tell.

One has a long pointed beard.
Can he be Santa Claus?
Next to him are the Picasso faces,
Who have features out of place.

When Nick was five years old
He saw the large wrinkled head of stone up high.
Nick said, "He died eleven-ten."
"How do you know?" I asked.
He replied, "I just do."

A year passed and I asked Nick when the head of stone died.
"He was the third person born. You know who the first two
    were."
"Adam and Eve" I replied.
"Yes, and he was the third person born."

The funniest heads are the chubby ones down low,
Dressed in colors of beige, orange, and blue.
Bushes grow behind their heads in wild array
As if to say, "I'm having a bad hair day."

Most elegant was the massive stone lion,
He was as majestic as the lion in Narnia.
And still, on another day, I saw
A bear across the stone wall.

Faces in the rims of Billings as viewed by Nick

The Best

The day has come to find the best one.
To Laurel and south we drive.
So that our wagon can hold
The best pumpkin in the patch.

Up and down each row we go,
Seeking, thumping, examining.
No blemish can you have,
The best pumpkin from the patch.

We find you and take you home,
The best one on the block,
To scoop out and carve your face
So you can scare those little beggars.

And now winter has come,
You lie shriveled and wrinkled.
But still I remember you,
The best pumpkin from the patch.

Strega Nona

After lunch at McDonalds,
Nanny and Nick will join his first-grade class
At the Alberta Bair Theater,
Where magic comes alive.

We find his classmates in front row center,
Among the many rows of excited school children.
The chatter feels deafening.
Then up comes the curtain.

Nick's eyes gaze upward above the stage
To the many spotlights in various colors.
He sits transfixed throughout,
With face so serious while others laugh.

They perform with exuberant enthusiasm,
Their voices blending beautifully,
Dancing, costumes, and sets, lively,
But Nick's gaze is on the lights so bright.

"How did you like the play?" I asked.
"It was awesome," he replied.
"I loved the pasta all over the stage.
I really wanted to eat some."
Back into the world we went
Where snow was falling steadily,
Just like it did when
Charlie went to *Grease* and Abbie to *The Nutcracker*.

Shirley Shirley

What joy it brings me
Taking grandchildren to the theater.
These are the best of times,
Grandchildren, the theater, and me.

Red Lodge Mountain

It was the most beautiful day.
Last night, Charlie, age eleven, called with a request for
Nanny, age seventy-six: "Will you take me skiing tomorrow?"
"Call me when you wake up and see how I feel.
And ask your mother if anyone else wants to go."

The day was again beautiful when he called back.
"It will be just you and me, Nanny, if we can go," he said.
We loaded the skis and headed to Red Lodge.
When we came to the scary mountain cliff drive,
Charlie kept me informed of where not to drive off the side,
Or we would surely die.

Ski boots on and tickets purchased we got on the
Triple lift chair to soar up the mountain.
After getting used to my new skis, I soon glide down like a
    graceful bird.
Charlie prefers speed, like being shot out of a cannon.
All day long, he would fly and I would glide, only to see each
    other at the bottom.

High on the mountain I viewed the distant mountains all
    blue and white.
I had never seen them so beautiful.
As we drove home with memories of the day, the clouds
    turned purple, the sky pink.
And in my rear view mirror was an orange sky above the ski
    runs. Such was our day on the mountain.

Thanksgiving 2011

I am thankful for prairies,
Their roots that go so deep,
For alpine tiny flowers
Upon the mountain peaks.

For strength to hike and ski
With my friends and family,
To share the many wonders
Given to you and me.

For every gift that comes from above
From the maker and keeper of our hearts,
May we always lift to Him,
Our wonder, thanks, and love.

Chapter 9:
God's Creation Gives Me Peace

The beauty in all His creation, from the tiniest to the massive mountains and sky, are daily joys.

You cannot remain in a depressed state very long when you get outside and thank the creator for all that is around you—well, most of it, anyway. Man has not always taken care of the natural world, but we can contribute to keeping the world beautiful.

In the same way, we can help others in cancer sharing our talents of knitting, writing, fishing, etc., to help them enjoy life and give them peace.

Elk Lake on the East Rosebud Trail
in the Beartooth Mountains

Dragonflies

Wings as fine as gauze,
Slender body shimmering in the sunlight.
The dragonfly lands
Close to where I am sitting.

"What big eyes you have," I say.
"All the better to see mosquitoes with,
For me to catch them in midair,
To have my lunch in midflight," it replies.

With all its beauty and color,
It then darted away so fast,
To escape birds and other prey,
To gladden someone else's day.

Morning Visitors

I sit at my breakfast table,
Pouring a cup of coffee.
Light is streaming through the east windows,
And then a flash of movement I see.

Two squirrels and then four scamper
Up and down the trees,
As if to say to each other,
"Catch me if you can."

They have the high-wire act down,
Like any circus performer,
Leaping from tree to tree,
Walking across telephone wires.

I hear their feet scamper across the roof.
The action I find amusing,
While I sit there in the morning,
Just drinking a cup of coffee.

Sounds

I close my eyes and listen to spring.
Winds are whistling in the pines;
They sound like water in a mountain stream.
Birds are chirping a happy song;
I think they are wrens, my husband's favorite.
An airplane takes off above the rims.
My white metal rocker sets up a rhythm.
The wind sounds increase, trying to stir up some rain.
I hear an animal and see a bunny hop into the Juniper.
My kitty purrs; the neighbors' dogs bark.
Until I listened, I thought it was quiet.

To See

Look all around you.
See what you can see;
The tiny lady bug,
The large oak tree.

I see their shapes,
How their colors blend together.
Then in the shadows
I see the patterns grow.

As I sit observing,
A friend comes up to me,
Making a comment on the scene,
Showing me more to see.

Together we share and
Our observations grow.
So much there is to see,
How much I didn't know.

The Cloud

From an airplane I have often wondered
What would it be like to walk on a cloud.
It looks so soft and bouncy,
Where you could have a wonderful time.

And then my chance came to be in a cloud when
Diane and I were skiing at Red Lodge Mountain.
While we were eating lunch in the midmountain chalet,
Diane said, "Look at the clouds coming in."

And so they did. The cloud moved down on the mountain.
Then I wondered, "Will I be able to see to ski?"
So down I skied through the cloud, and could now answer,
   "No problem."

As Diane rode up the ski lift in the cloud,
Suddenly, she came out of the cloud and appeared in the
   sunlight.
It was like a miracle, like a trip to heaven,
Traveling through that cloud.

Fresh Snow

I love the fresh snow
So white and pure,
Like a newborn
With skin so soft.

It speaks of renewal,
Of time to start anew
In those life pursuits
We haven't found time to do.

We can go to the
Attics of our minds
In the stillness of winter
To find hidden treasures.

Winter Colors

The first white snow is falling,
On the evergreens and pines.
The sky is grey
On this winter day.
But along the rims,
A few red berries, I see, and
Touches of orange and gold.

Nature is slowed and sleeping
Giving us rest and reflection
Remembering the times we have had,
The seasons of our past.

A White Winter Day

Pheasants are feeding in the backyard,
Their feathers of turquoise, wine, and gold,
Shining in the sunlight,
On this white, winter day.

From snow-covered hills,
Four birds peck below our pines,
Finding a spot of barren earth
Where seeds have dropped.

I'll throw out some red corn
To add to their food,
And further enjoy their bright colors
On this white, winter day.

Chapter 10:
The Journey Brings Fulfillment

In my study of Psalms, I noticed the last five chapters begin with "Praise the Lord." Many of the early Psalms state a time of struggle, but the book ends in praise.

I encourage you to keep a journal and write about your journey. The blessings multiply as you look back and see the patterns unfold on what God has given you.

The journey brings fulfillment in the Beartooth Mountains. Photo taken in the meadow above Greenough Lake with view of the Hellroaring Plateau on the Parkside National Recreational Trail.

Cancer has given me more reason to appreciate the simple joys in life and the importance of family, friends, ministers, and caregivers. I start each day with a new appreciation for all I have been given, including cancer, and to give thanks. The journey has been good, and I know it has brought a special fulfillment in my Christian life—like no other experience could.

Psalm of Blessing

The Lord is my light and salvation,
Whom shall I fear?
I am not afraid.
My confidence is in you.

I ask Oh Lord,
That I may dwell in your house
All the days of my life,
To gaze upon your beauty.

In the day of trouble
You will keep me safe,
Hide me in your shelter
And set me high upon a rock.
Above my enemies and fears
I will cast my eyes upon You.
I will sing and make music to the Lord.

I know you will never reject me.
Teach me your ways, O Lord.
Lead me in the straight path.

"You have made known to me the path of life;
You will fill me with joy in your presence,
With eternal pleasures at your right hand."[25]

May I see the goodness of the Lord
Here, each day, in Montana.
I wait on you, Lord,
Make me strong.
Take my heart that waits on You.[26]

The Rock

The rocks in the Beartooth Mountains
Are so vast and varied—
What a tumult their arrival
Must have been.

I see in them terror and strength
Beyond what I can imagine,
A high tower out of the dark valley,
Rising up to the clear blue sky.

The trail is uncertain
But I lift my eyes
To the great "I AM."

He will not let my foot slip.
"The Lord is the stronghold of my life—
Of whom shall I be afraid?"[27]

He will keep me safe
And hold my right hand.
I will sing and make music to the Lord.

The Journey

Help me remember the journey.
How You helped me in good times and bad.
Through sunshine and rain,
You supported me.

Each day I give You thanks,
Not just a simple thank you,
But one rejoicing
With song and praise.

Set me high upon a rock.
Let me dwell on the mountaintop
To be with You on high,
To give You thanks and praise.

Biography: Shirley A. Shirley

In 1994, Shirley illustrated and wrote the book *Restoring the Tallgrass Prairie*, which is still in publication.

Shirley graduated with a BS degree in nursing from the University of Iowa, Iowa City.

In addition to sketching native plants, she also paints in pastel and watercolor. Her creativity also extended to designing needlework for the national market during the sixteen years she owned a yarn shop.

Shirley now creates copper jewelry and takes metalwork classes taught by Mark Moak at Rocky Mountain College in Billings, Montana. Her jewelry is sold at festivals and is represented in thirteen galleries in five states.

She grew up in Des Moines, Iowa, and with her husband raised four children in Eldora, Iowa, a town of three thousand near the Iowa River and Pine Lake State Park. On Halloween in 2008, Shirley, her husband, Dr. Robert Shirley, and their cat, Bunny, moved from the prairies of Iowa to the mountains of Montana to be near one of their daughter's family of five children. In addition to the joy she finds in them, Shirley has found the Red Lodge Hiking Club in the Beartooth Mountains and Bible Study Fellowship in Billings rewarding.

Words from this author: "As a teenager I chose as my life verse Psalm 16:11: 'You have made known to me the path of life; you will fill me with joy in your presence, with eternal pleasures at your right hand.' The Lord Jesus Christ has never failed me. He is my salvation, the strength of my life.

"I find refuge, strength, gratitude, and joy in writing for all I have been given—including cancer. In poetry, I find a rhythm and quality of life supporting me in the difficult times and in hope for the future."

Bible Endnote References

1.   Joshua 1:9b

2.   Hebrews 13:5b

3.   John 8:12

4.   James 1:17

5.   2 Corinthians 12:10b

6.   Psalm 121:1-2

7.   Romans 8: 26b – 27b

8.   Paraphrased from Psalm 46:10a

9.   Paraphrased from Judges 6-7

10.   Paraphrased from Judges 6:23-24

11.   Ecclesiastes 1:18

12.   Ecclesiastes 3:1, 4

13.   Ecclesiastes 7:12b-13a

14.   Ecclesiastes 7:14

15.   Matthew 11: 28-30

16.   Esther 4:16b

17.   Psalm 118:24

18.   Paraphrased from Psalm 150

19.   Based on Matthew 7:7

20.   Paraphrased from Revelation 21:23

21.   Paraphrased from Revelation 22:1

22.   Similar truth as found in refining gold,
        Revelation   3:18a

23.   Based on John 4:10

24.   Based on Psalm 23

25.   Psalm 16:11

26.   Paraphrased from Psalm 27

27.   Psalm 27:2